FIVE SUBSTANTIAL
STEPS
and MORE...
FOR SUCCESS
in the
WORLD OF SALES

- -

FAISAL BINALI

ISBN
978-1-5437-5192-5 (sc)
978-1-5437-5193-2 (e)

Print information available on the last page.

To order additional copies of this book, contact
Toll Free 800 101 2657 (Singapore)
Toll Free 1 800 81 7340 (Malaysia)
www.partridgepublishing.com/singapore
orders.singapore@partridgepublishing.com

06/12/2019

PARTRIDGE

Fear Allah wherever you are; follow up a bad deed with a good deed and it will wipe it out; and behave with people in a good manner.

—Prophet Muhammad

To my father and mother, may Allah SWT bless and protect them, as a simple expression of my deep and unconditional love.

To my beloved wife and companion, who stood by and supported me throughout my journey in life.

To my children, the gifts that Allah SWT blessed me with, AbdulAllah and AlSamiyah.

To my dear brother, Dr Sultan.

To everyone I had the privilege and honour to train, and to all those who are enthusiastic about the world of sales and customer service and who hope to accomplish something valuable in this world.

Contents

Preface

This book is directed to my dear friends who wish to be innovators and achievers in their careers in the world of sales. It contains a brief extract of my previous professional experience. I began my career in the public sector as a writing clerk at the procurement and contract management department. In the private sector, I started out as a salesman for a company that specialises in the products and services of mobile phones. I gradually progressed to the following positions:

- o Branch Supervisor
- o Sales Support Specialist
- o Commercial Operations Specialist (Customers)
- o Senior Quality Assurance Specialist
- o Sales Director of the Eastern Province
- o Commercial Operations Specialist (Corporate)
- o Marketing and Development Consultant for the Development of Landline Packages and Fibre Optics

In all the above, one of my main duties—besides managing projects, contributing to the development of new companies in the Saudi market, and innovating and developing products and services—was to honourably and proudly train salespeople across various career levels, including salespersons, supervisors, and regional managers, in both the individual sales sector and the corporate and business sales sector.

I have never been more proud of anyone as much as I have been with the salesmen, who are sometimes referred to as sales representatives or sales consultants, whom I've had the honour and privilege of teaching. I truly thank them for all I have learned from their comments and questions during training sessions that I have prepared to guide them in their initial steps in the private sector and in the world of sales.

Who Is the Client?

Many definitions have been put forward to attempt to describe a client and his or her relationship with a salesperson of a company, regardless of the salesperson's specific position and duties. I outline the definition as follows.

A client is the person who pays our salaries, from the company's chairperson to the salesperson. The client is the one who grants us the social welfare we receive from the companies we work for, in exchange for the client's satisfaction and acceptance of our products and services that fully cater to the client's needs. The client is the reason behind the company's profits, its continuation, and the success of its future investments.

The client is the actual owner of the company for which you work. However, out of respect, the client is classified as your partner and guest who accepts nothing other than what is positive and favourable.

The Client's Privileges

Clients have certain privileges that give them their well-deserved value. Such privileges include the following:

- ✓ accepting all their objections
- ✓ understanding that we will never be successful unless the clients are fully satisfied

And remember the following:

- ✓ Losing clients imposes a threat to the company.
- ✓ We need clients more than they need us.
- ✓ Clients are friends; their satisfaction is our goal, and keeping them is our aim.
- ✓ Our future depends on our clients' satisfaction.
- ✓ The clients are the reason behind keeping your job as a salesperson and keeping the company operating as a for-profit organisation.
- ✓ The clients have the absolute freedom of choosing whatever they want. It is your duty as a salesperson to provide them with the alternatives that best suit their needs.
- ✓ You are the one who best understands the clients' needs; they will accept nothing other than what exceeds their expectations.
- ✓ You were not chosen by the clients in order to assure them that they did the right thing by choosing your company; they chose you to prove to them that choosing you and your company was right thing to do.
- ✓ Clients should be free to choose any method or approach when communicating with us. Your duty is to accept this and deal positively with all their behaviours and attitudes.

✓ Clients have the absolute right to reject and criticise us. You, on the other hand, have all the skills and expertise necessary to turn this into an opportunity to foster your relationship with existing clients and create relationships with new ones.

Sales: The Concept

Sales is a collection of positive outcomes (profits, benefits, interests, relationships, etc.) that results from a specific consultative relationship between a salesperson and a prospective or existing client who is considering a product or a service provided by a company through this salesperson. This product or service should satisfy or exceed the needs and expectations of the client.

Sales is a prestigious and respected career that does not include:

o temptation
o persuasion
o lying
o falsifying facts
o harming the client after purchasing the product or service

Sales is about building long-term relationships that are based on honesty, trust, loyalty, and commitment to providing our clients with their needs and requirements. For this reason, we salespeople are considered consultants to our clients.

The Definition of *Sale* in Arabic Glossaries

Sale (noun)
Plural: Sales.
Source: Sell.
Perform a Sale: Accomplish it fully.

It is a transaction that includes the exchange of a commodity for another or for something of an equal value. Buying and selling is performed in markets: 'Men whom neither trade nor sales diverts them from the Remembrance of Allah' (Surat Al-Noor 37).

Voluntary Sale: A sale conducted liberally or freely.

Sale Allowance: A reduction in the price charged by a seller.

(Kifaya) Adequacy Sale: For instance, you owe Zaid five dirhams, and you purchase something from Amr worth five dirhams as well, so you ask Amr to take this money from Zaid.

Auction Sale: The public sale of something to the highest bidder.

Cost-Plus Financing (Murabaha) Sale (Economics): Selling goods at a price plus an agreed-upon profit markup or margin.

Exchange Sale (Economics): Purchasing bonds from a market to sell them immediately in another market.

Exposure Sale (Economics): Selling stocks or bonds borrowed from a person prior to their profit, and paying for them only after the price goes down.

Sales Contract (Economics): A contract between two parties, the seller and the buyer, whereby the seller is committed to release his ownership of a particular commodity, and the buyer is committed to paying the price of this commodity.

No Selling and no Buying: A phrase usually used to describe a recession in the market.

Bayi' (noun)
Al-Bayi': The seller.
Al-Bayi': The negotiator.
Al-Bayi': A person skilled in sales.

The Most Widely Known Types or Methods of *Sale*s

1. Cross-Selling

Selling products and services that are not directly related in terms of composition to the product or service being sold to the customer.

Benefits of Cross-Selling

- ✓ providing an added value to the main products or services
- ✓ increasing the profits of the company for which you work
- ✓ widening your client base because of their trust in your ability to provide them with all they need
- ✓ increasing customer loyalty to the company, as well as the loyalty of their friends and relatives
- ✓ supporting the development of the products and services of the company for which you work
- ✓ making the client the primary salesperson for all your products
- ✓ selling multiple products and services in a single transaction
- ✓ increasing clients' confidence in your ability to provide them with what they need
- ✓ improving the status of your company and its reputation of caring for its clients' needs

2. Upselling

Upselling is a selling technique in which the customer is given add-on benefits, services, or additional products that are directly or indirectly related to the main products and services sold. This added benefit and value will be provided for only a nominal fee.

Benefits of Upselling

1. supporting the company for which you work
2. improving customer loyalty and devotion
3. allowing the customer the chance to save some money
4. increasing the opportunity of marketing for all products and services
5. increasing the profits of the company for which you work
6. increasing the chance that a client will select your company, rather than one of your competitors
7. increasing your popularity and keeping in line with the needs of your clients
8. making the clients the primary salespeople for all your products
9. selling and presenting multiple products and services in a single transaction
10. providing clients with the chance of owning products and services that they might need later for a lower price
11. providing maximum benefit to clients at an affordable cost should they wish to have an extra product, service, value, or benefit

The Characteristics of a Highly Successful Salesperson

Successful Salespeople are confident individuals who love their career and perform it with the utmost professionalism and pleasure in order to gain new customers and create a client base for themselves as well as for the company for which they work. They have certain personality traits, such as the following:

* Being calm, understanding, and well-informed.
* The ability to listen well to clients.
* The ability to negotiate and cooperate.
* A love of helping and serving all people.
* Honesty, loyalty, and trustworthiness.
* Respect for other points of view.
* Strong loyalty and faithfulness towards clients and the company for which they work.
* As salespeople, they are considered the most important employees at the company.
* The ability to deal with complaints and objections.
* Discussing benefits and interests with his clients before bringing up the subject of money/price.
* Maintaining an ongoing advisory and friendly relationship with the client.

- ❖ Being organised and taking good care of themselves, their surroundings, and the place in which they work.
- ❖ Always being on the hunt for information, and loving to discover and explore.
- ❖ A smile is an essential and inseparable part of their personality, life, and the language of their bodies and souls.
- ❖ They do not persuade customers into buying products or services. Instead, they sell them what they need through consultative selling and by providing them with alternatives.
- ❖ Continuing to serve clients welcomingly with all their ability, attention, and effort, even after the clients receive the product/service, in order to keep them satisfied and to encourage future sales.
- ❖ Continuing to serve clients—even those who refused to purchase the product or service. They do so welcomingly with all their ability, attention, and effort in order to keep clients satisfied and create an opportunity to actually do the sale.

The Sixteen Privileges of the Sales Profession:

Sales is a profession that generously provides for those who love it and hope to work in its field. It has several privileges, such as the following:

1. Easily marketing for oneself.
2. The total absence of routine.
3. Control over the level of income.
4. Satisfaction and self-development.
5. Social status and social relationships.
6. Freedom of using skills and abilities.
7. Pleasure in facing daily challenges.
8. A promising future and excellent income possibilities.
9. Building new relationships in all areas.
10. Keeping a constant smile and mastering negotiation skills.
11. Ease of switching jobs and moving from one company to another.
12. Every day is considered a true addition to one's experience and career.
13. Always pushing the salesperson into caring for and developing oneself and one's relationships.
14. Enjoying one's accomplishments and successes after realising one's sales goals or winning a new client.
15. A main reason for developing the knowledge and information of the salesman is that the sales career constantly encourages research, discovery, and evaluation.
16. There is no limit for how innovative or creative a salesperson can become. It is the profession that is most supportive of continuous creativity and innovation.

The Rights of the Client

Committing to your duties towards your clients means that you and the company you work for are committed to the optimal route for your future success in the world of sales.

Such duties include the following:

❖ The clients deserve trust.
❖ The clients deserve honesty.
❖ The clients deserve the freedom to choose.
❖ The clients deserve us to be committed to our duties towards them.
❖ Because they chose us, the clients will always deserve the best.
❖ The clients deserve to be totally satisfied with everything we provide them.
❖ The clients deserve to have his culture, interests, and affiliations respected, no matter what they are.
❖ The clients deserve to have their needs understood and identified. We should provide them with what would enable them to satisfy those needs, and not to persuade them into buying what we want to sell.

The Truth about Client Satisfaction

Everything that we or our companies do should be for the purpose of earning and rightfully deserving the satisfaction of our clients. They should not have anything to do with 'persuading' the client to remain with us.

Client satisfaction is an inevitable result of the high quality and honesty in what you present to your clients. To succeed in obtaining client satisfaction means that you have, both directly and indirectly, created a large client base with long-term relationships. This is the ultimate success for yourself as a salesman as well as for the company for which you work.

The Most Important Influences That Affect the Choices and Needs of Our Customers Today:

The following are the most important influences that affect the choices of our clients nowadays as they explore what suits their needs. You have to be aware of those influences and acquire the necessary skills and knowledge that will help you manage your relationship with your clients accordingly.

- ✓ a rise in aspirations and expectations
- ✓ a rise in the clients' education and knowledge level
- ✓ an increasing attachment with the products and services provided by companies
- ✓ a rise in the level of income and a variation in clients' personal commitments
- ✓ more free time and more areas of professional and personal interests
- ✓ the clients' ability to easily compare between those products or services produced locally and those produced abroad
- ✓ an increase in the clients' different sources of income, and their relationship with the products and services you provide

The Truth about a Salesman

A salesman is, directly and indirectly, a source of pride for both the company as well as the clients. When the salesman commits to his duties and obligations to reach his ambitions, he is actually accomplishing much for himself, his clients, and his company, even though those accomplishments may not be clearly identifiable. The outcomes of his commitments are invested in by his clients as well as by the company for which he works.

In committing to his principles, identity, and belonging to the world of sales, a salesman is considered a great person. The following proves his importance and value:

1. His is the active link between providing clients with what they need and the company's determination to provide the best products and services to its clients.
2. He is the one who supports the development of products and services according to the needs of the clients. By keeping his clients satisfied, he is also supporting the continuing success of the company.
3. He is the primary source, after Allah SWT blessings, for the rise in the profits of the company he works for, as well as for the happiness of clients with whom he was honest in providing what suits their needs.
4. He provides an accurate study about the products and services that he markets and sells in the following main areas:
   - What are they characterised with?
   - What are the actual benefits of their use?
   - What is their competitive advantage?
   - The reality of customer satisfaction—what are the aspects or characteristics that the products/services should have?
   - What are their flaws/defects?
   - What are the weak areas that should be developed?
   - What are the strong points that we should emphasise to the clients?
   - Who is the first person able to test and examine the products or services?
   - How can clients evaluate their prices, in terms of use as well as acquired benefit after consumption?

5. He understands the market in which the company he works for operates; he determines the different aspects on which they can compete.
6. He can predict and actively contribute in establishing or developing policies, plans, products, or services.
7. He represents the actual company, with all its potentials, values, and commitments, towards its clients and the market in which it operates.
8. He can achieve the company's strategic purposes and contribute to the success of the company. He can also be the reason for its failure.
9. Immediate response through following and monitoring his personal performance as well as the performance of his team, in addition to the immediate replying to the clients' comments or complaints.
10. He actively contributes to developing performance in all areas, including marketing, products, services, selecting locations, in addition to activities that foster relationships with clients and generate profit.

The Nine Fundamentals of Being a Salesperson

These fundamentals explain the methodology and framework that a salesperson should follow. Even if he has to perform his work on a daily basis, he should work out of passion and love for the world of sales. That is, he is not merely an employee whose job is to sell a product or a service. On the other hand, he is passionate about the world of sales, and he strongly hopes to succeed to achieve the highest possible income level and attain the highest possible career position in this field.

The fundamentals are explained in most training courses or related writings or texts. However, I will outline some that I work with and adopt in my work:

1. Knowing and trusting that you are the main element of the success of for-profit organisations.
2. Always seeking to build a lasting relationship with the client.
3. Understanding that the client does not simply purchase a commodity from you; he actually shares your interest and chooses to have you as a friend.
4. Making sure that you are well-versed with all aspects of the products/services that you are trying to sell, in addition to the real benefits of their use.
5. Acquiring the skills required to accomplish your goal, according to the highest standards and without jeopardising your clients' trust.
6. Serving the needs of older people and people with special needs, and doing so in the best way possible and with utmost respect.
7. Motivating clients to switch to what is better for them. However, beware of pushing clients into purchasing products or services that do not suit their needs.
8. Having the ability to utilise your skills to perform better, and accomplishing this in the proper time frame while keeping respect for the time of your clients.

9. Caring for your personal appearance and your positive attitude, whether in the presence or in the absence of your team members or clients. Organising your work place and making sure it is clean at all times will provide you with the best environment to speak with and have discussions with your clients.

The Dual Loyalty of a Salesman

This topic addresses one of the most difficult issues that a salesman faces in his work, since he must use all his skills, abilities, and information to compromise between the directions and goals of the company he works for while at the same time committing to his duties towards his clients, as explained earlier. The need for his professional skills and abilities become even more important when there is a conflict between the clients and the company. This means that a salesman has to succeed in managing this conflict while holding on to his loyalty towards both his current or future clients as well as to the company he works for and represents.

Managing this dual loyalty with honesty and mutual trust is one of the key elements of the success of a salesman. The more capable he is of managing his loyalties in an effective and positive way, the closer he is to achieving his goals in the world of sales.

It is important to note that dual loyalty becomes more or less intense according to the importance of customer satisfaction to the decision makers and people working at the company.

- What does the client represent to the company?
- Is customer satisfaction a primary goal that the company dedicates all its resources to achieve, or is it only a secondary goal?
- Where, in the priorities of the company, does customer satisfaction (and giving them what exceeds their expectations) lie?

The Daily Duties of a Salesman (the Fourteen Accomplishments)

The daily duties of a salesman are considered real accomplishments if performed with honesty and genuine belief in their importance for the company and the client. The salesman is the link between the two most important factors: the success of the company and the satisfaction of its client. The most important duties of a salesman include the following:

1. determining the needs of the clients
2. finding and winning new clients
3. resolving clients' complaints
4. accentuating himself, his abilities, and his potentials
5. providing help and support to the clients

6. serving his clients and promoting the company
7. marketing for himself as well as the products and services of the company
8. discovering more factors that increase client satisfaction
9. representing the company he works for in the best possible way
10. submitting studies that analyse the status of the market as well as the company's competitors
11. discovering factors that affect the development and innovation of products and services
12. fostering positive relationships to support himself and the company in the future
13. determining any defects in the systems and procedures or products and services
14. providing studies that explain the strong and weak points of the company's products and services and those of its competitors

Beware of the Following: A Spotlight on the 'Absolutely' Nonpositive Sides in Managing the Relationship with Current or Prospective Clients

1. Never allow the sales target that you are required to achieve interfere with how you manage your relationship with clients, no matter what difficulties or pressures you face to achieve those targets. Doing so will push you to involuntarily make huge mistakes with your clients, which lead to really bad outcomes, such as:
   - Selling the client a commodity that he does not need.
   - Losing the client's trust, which means losing your next opportunity.
   - Inability to understand and comprehend what the client's real needs are.
   - The loss of positive marketing, both for yourself as well as for the products and services with which you provide the client.
   - Switching your goal from gaining customer satisfaction to solely achieving the required sales target.
   - Providing the client with wrong alternatives, because your focus is not on supplying the client with what he needs and what is proper for him; all you want is to accomplish sell and end the deal.
   - Losing future clients; losing a client for any of the reasons mentioned above means that any friend or relative of this client who might have been a prospective client will never go through this experience with you.
   - The client has nothing to do neither with your personal life nor with your administrative relationship with the company that you work for. Such matters should never be used to start a conversation with a client or to manage a relationship with him.

2. The client did not approach you to discuss your issues or problems with the company for which you work. Any discussion in this topic will have a direct effect on the client's

trust, both in you and in the company you represent. Topics and actions that should be avoided include the following:

- Comparing your company with other companies.
- Blaming your company for any dereliction of duty towards the client or yourself.
- Topics that do not support the relationship with the client.
- Criticising the company for making a decision that does not work well or is unfair to you.
- Having a 'negative' attitude when criticising your company in front of the client. Instead, be conservative and responsible. Although you seek to satisfy your customers and understand their needs, you still are representing this company.

3. In no way should you discuss the weaknesses of your competitors. Rather, expertly focus on what you own, the benefits of your products and services, and the values they can provide to the client.

Do Not Be like the Following People, for They Are Not True Salesmen

- o a dishonest salesman
- o a salesman who exploits his company or clients
- o an ignorant salesman who knows nothing about the market in which his company operates
- o a salesman with a stiff attitude towards his clients and colleagues
- o a salesman who cannot be trusted by his clients and colleagues
- o a salesman who does not respect the culture of others and does not accept the differences between people
- o a salesman who is ignorant of the advantages and disadvantages of what he wants to market and sell
- o a salesman whose loyalty is for a company other than the one for which he works
- o a salesman who does not wish to work in sales but is 'forced' to do so
- o a salesman who works only to achieve his sales target, rather than establishing foundations with which he can achieve those targets

Words to Avoid

There are certain words that a salesman must avoid because of the negative effect they might have on his relationship with his clients. Such words can be the reason behind the poor management of those relationships. The words may express a commitment or a promise that the salesman cannot fulfil, even if he tries his best. Furthermore, they might highlight the role that other departments, such as the customer service department's service centre, have in managing the client's relationship with the salesman. Any shortcoming in the operation of those departments would mean that the salesman did not commit to his word or promise. Moreover, the words might touch on bad experiences that the client previously had with other companies. Such words might cause the client to start losing trust in company.

Thus, to maintain respect and trust between the salesperson, the company he works for, and his clients, certain words that have negative indications or nonpositive future effects must be avoided. Such words include the following:

- o I will try to get for you …
  You have to do all what you are capable of in order to fulfil your promises to the clients and earn their satisfaction.

- o I am not actually sure.
  If you are unsure of something, then you should ask the team member who knows the right information without letting your client notice; otherwise, you will lose his trust very early on.

- o It is not my fault.
  Never run away from your responsibilities. Although a problem or mistake may be outside your job scope, the client has put his trust in you, not in anyone else.

- o Our prices are the lowest.
  Clients know very well what products and services are available in the market, what their prices are, and what benefits/values they will receive in return to the price they pay, and whether this price is higher or lower than what's available in the market or of the competitors. Thus, always focus on the competing products or services without undermining what is offered by competing companies.

- o Always.
  There is nothing that occurs, whether in our personal or professional lives, that we can claim is 'constantly happening'. This is the case throughout the whole world, in the smallest as well as the biggest of all matters. The world is changing at a very rapid pace.

- o Never.
  Do not use words that indicate definite acceptance or rejection. Everything in the world is changing at a very quick speed, especially in competing markets where there is more than one company producing goods and services on a daily basis.

- o What you need is …
  Do not specify to the clients what they need. Simply provide them with alternatives that are compatible with and close to their needs. Clients are highly educated and informed, and they have the freedom to choose what they want.

- o Trust me.

Never ask for trust. Always be capable of earning it through:

- your pleasant behaviour, which stems from your morals and ethics and by speaking clearly and transparently about any topic discussed
- being truthful in everything you say
- fulfilling your promises

A Salesman Is a Person with Good Morals and Values

This is contrary to the widespread view that a salesman is only a means for marketing products or services, or merely a method by which companies communicate with their clients, or that he is that employee who simply cares for selling a product and nothing else, or any other view (whether positive or negative) that undermines the salesman and his morals and ethics.

My dear salesman, you have to understand and believe that you are a man of morals and values, and that there are principles that cannot be compromised no matter how difficult your personal life or work conditions become. Know for sure that if you do not believe so, you are definitely on the wrong path of success in the world of sales, and that even if you achieve temporary success, you will be losing the right path for a continuous and lasting success.

The Most Important Morals and Values in the Life of a Salesman

- ❖ loyalty
- ❖ affiliation
- ❖ ambition
- ❖ honesty
- ❖ fidelity
- ❖ trustfulness
- ❖ integrity
- ❖ cooperation
- ❖ patience
- ❖ humility
- ❖ confidence
- ❖ sincerity
- ❖ respect for others
- ❖ investigation and discovery

The Personal Traits of an Excellent Salesman

Those traits are closely connected with the abilities and skills of the salesperson, although some often debate whether those traits are innate or whether they can be acquired by training.

However, from my personal experience, I believe that even what is innate has to be refined by training, and what is not can be learnt and acquired.

The Most Important Personal Traits

- ❖ self-confidence
- ❖ taking responsibilities
- ❖ creativity and innovation
- ❖ skilled in negotiation
- ❖ expert in meeting and dealing with audiences
- ❖ committing to deadlines and what needs to be accomplished within the set time
- ❖ organising his own self and his workplace
- ❖ accepting challenges and finding alternatives to overcome them
- ❖ providing substitutes that are most compatible with the needs
- ❖ expertise in using emerging technologies and its tools
- ❖ desire to develop any weak areas in one's personality or performance
- ❖ skilled in consultative selling, not in persuasive selling
- ❖ expert in dealing with complaints and objections, in addition to compliments
- ❖ understanding the importance of sharing information and discussing daily matters with team members
- ❖ genuine desire to teach others, transfer one's expertise to them, and give them advice and guidance

The Twenty Fundamentals for Success in the World of Sales

There are many fundamentals for success in the world of sales. They are considered indispensable prerequisites for the excellence and success of a salesman. The twenty most important ones are as follows:

1. confident and capable of handling responsibilities
2. has a genuine smile and a love for work
3. elegant and cares for his personal hygiene
4. well-informed and versed with all aspects of what is presented to clients
5. utilises his potentials and skills in the most optimal way, and continuously develops and improves his abilities

6. has a strong passion for competing with himself as well as with his colleagues who work in the same field
7. has the ambition to achieve more profit for his company and improve his personal income
8. able to reassure clients and earn their trust
9. has the desire to and enjoys helping clients, even after working hours
10. cares for the arrangement and cleanliness of his surroundings as well as his workplace
11. carefully observes and evaluates what is best for the needs of the clients
12. never ceases to improve his knowledge, enrich his education and culture, and read about what is new
13. always enthusiastic about making his company's name widely known, and always keen on increasing his client base
14. never worries about achieving his sales target, and always finds ways to accomplish what is required on time
15. works for earning his clients' trust, as opposed to manipulating or persuading them into buying something that would not satisfy their needs
16. failure does not hinder or despair him; rather, he regards it as the first step to accomplishing future achievements
17. keen on keeping continuous communication going with his clients, and maintaining a friendly relationship with them even if this did not result in a sales deal or operation
18. does not allow his personal problems or problems he has with his company to interfere with his relationship with clients or in the way he serves his current or prospective clients
19. is always prepared to do his best to serve and guide his clients after the sales deal is done, giving them advice about any new products or services
20. always able to transform rejections, complaints, and objections into opportunities result in successful sales operations

The Ten Principal Competencies in Problem-Solving and Finding Alternatives

A salesman never gives up. He knows very well how to overcome difficulties and remove any barriers to his personal success or the success of the company he represents, or anything that stands in the way of earning the satisfaction of his clients. For this reason, I believe the following are the basic competencies that a salesperson should have to be able to solve problems and find alternatives, and to continue moving on the path towards success and accomplishments:

1. analysing reasons
2. solving problems
3. recognising the presence of a problem
4. determining the problem and reasons behind it
5. choosing only one solution for the problem
6. determining the best solutions according to available resources

7. evaluating and trying a number of solutions, and examining the results
8. determining the available resources to solve the problem
9. working towards eliminating the sources of the problem to avoid its recurrence
10. acknowledging the accepted solution and adopting it in solving any similar problems in the future

The Clients' Concept of an Objection

A salesperson must realise that objections do have several positive aspects, including the following:

1. a perfect selling opportunity
2. a chance to improve the level of client satisfaction
3. an essential reason behind building a new relationship
4. understanding the strong areas and developing and improving the weak areas
5. an opportunity for the salesperson to train, develop, and utilise one's selling skills
6. an opportunity to promote to the client the company's products and services
7. an objecting client with whom you are able to build or renew a successful relationship will be more loyal to you in the future if you were able to properly solve his problem

From the above, we can put forth a general definition of an objection. It is a reaction or method of expression that clients use to convey their dissatisfaction or disapproval of a particular product or service. In addition, it is considered a way of expressing their feelings about the company's dereliction of duties. It is also a way to discover how well the clients understand the product or service and the benefits of its use. It is considered an offensive behaviour, regardless of how friendly it seems.

Types and Causes of Objections

Below, I combine both the most common types of objections along with their causes. The list contains only some of the examples of such objections. However, it is important to note that a client is able to use more than one type simultaneously.

Logical Objections

The reasons and causes to object are genuine and clear. The discussion usually revolves around:

o the client not understanding the product
o the client not understanding the service
o poor after-sales customer service
o not committing to providing the promised features and benefits

Illogical Objections

There's no logical reason behind the objection. He is merely objecting early on during discussions for a few possible reasons:

- o to get an extra discount
- o to get more features and benefits
- o because it is the client's usual behaviour or attitude
- o to get extra free features or services
- o it might simply be a result of a client's personal behaviour or attitude
  ** If you are able to provide the client with extra features or benefits, then do so. Do not wait for the client to object in order to give them.

Emotional or Behavioural Objections

These are connected to the nature of the client's behaviour. We can focus on the most common types of such customers, because usually the reason behind their objections is due to a conflict with their nature. This includes the following:

- o lack of respect towards the nature of older people
- o being slow with people who are constantly in a hurry
- o not committing to your word with people who are decision-makers
- o not interacting with people who always seem angry
- o not expressing your admiration for egotistic people

Indirect Objections

The following causes of objections are not directly related to you as a salesman. On the other hand, the client is asking you for solutions or expressing his opinion to you. He is certain that you will either help him or at least show interest for his opinions, and that you will take the proper course of action in either case (which is a duty of a salesman). Here are some examples:

- o The advertisements of the company are inappropriate.
- o The product or service price is higher than that of the competitor.
- o The product or service is incompatible with something he already has.
- o There are no parking spaces or air conditioning available in the selling location; it is inappropriate.
- o He has not been served well by customer service while using the toll-free phone numbers.
- o The services are poor during certain times of the day or in certain conditions, such as weather, modern houses, terrains, or work locations.

Verbal or Negotiable Objections

Those are the strategies followed in managing discussions. They are used by a client to support his objections or prove his point of view, or even to control the discussion in a way that serves his view. Such objections are manifested through certain actions such as:

o   directly interrupting the speaker or asking for the chance to talk
o   a switch in the body language every now and then and after making the objection, like the movement of the hands and the way of sitting
o   trying to involve external influences, such as presenting proofs from marketing flyers or text messages in the client's phone
o   trying to logically demonstrate the objection—for instance, by calling the customer service toll-free number during the discussion, reading out monthly bills, or trying out a feature that does not work

Principles of Dealing with Objections

❖   Do not face the objection. Instead, engage in it.
❖   The client is right. We are the ones to blame and the ones who are not doing their jobs right.
❖   Understand the causes and reasons behind the objection. Then fix any problems.
❖   Take necessary actions to eliminate the causes and reasons behind the objections.
❖   Never allow objections to be a reason for losing your clients.
❖   Consider it the shortest path to show attention and serious interest in helping your clients.
❖   After understanding and dealing with the objections, try to understand the customer's attitude and deal with it.
❖   Do not let those reasons and causes lead to future objections.
❖   Deal with the objection, but at the same time preserve the rights of your client. Also maintain your respect and appreciation for him.
❖   Listen carefully to your client. Trying to quickly calm down the client or end the problem should not make you lose your active listening skills.
❖   Be careful not to promise the client to solve his problem in order to earn his temporary satisfaction. Instead, promise to take the necessary corrective actions.
❖   Try to anticipate any possible complaints that might come up when releasing a new product or service. Rely on your experience; it is your greatest support tool.

Understanding Body Language

Body language has become a science that includes several specialties. In general, we can define body language as all the conscious and unconscious positions, movements, gestures, and signals of the different body parts, such as hand or facial expressions, tone of the voice, look of the eye, movement of the eyebrow, and more. They represent reactions to specific incidents or express certain psychological states. They can also be a method of explaining something or welcoming someone.

They are important because they impact the way we communicate with others. They are especially important to a salesman because people react to and interact with body movements and ways of talking more than they do with actual spoken words.

Body Language and the *Sales*man

A salesman must be an expert in understanding body language and its implications, benefits, and drawbacks. He should also be able to control it. Reading the body language of others is one of the key factors and is a major tool behind the success of a salesman in various areas, such as:

o   customer service
o   managing relationships with clients
o   making a positive first impression with clients
o   dealing with different types of clients

Body Language That Should Be Avoided

Unsuitable body language at an inappropriate time, such as:

o   a broad smile with an angry client
o   mocking a way of speaking, or keeping eye contact with a shy or arrogant client

Unacceptable tone of voice, such as:

o   a hasty tone with a calm client
o   a provocative tone with a client who is only visiting

Folding arms in a defensive manner, such as:

o   Not being patient with a talkative client who asks many questions.
o   Not accepting a client with a harsh behaviour, and not being able to deal with him professionally.
o   Expressing lack of desire to listen and being overly defensive and close-minded. Always keep your hands open by your side to show that you are listening attentively and that you have an open mind for discussion.

Sitting or positioning your body behind the table or very close to the client, such as:

o focusing on the computer screen while speaking to an older client
o organising papers, pens, or other stationary while speaking with an outgoing or positive client
o getting closer than an arm's distance while speaking to a client; this is a huge mistake

Touching the client, such as:

o Do not shake the hands of an angry client or hold his hands while trying to convince him to sit down so that you can understand the problem.
o Do not be impulsively touch any belongings of an egoistic client while trying to show your liking for her, like touching her pen, watch, or mobile phone.

Negative facial expressions, such as:

o Do not bite your lips or widen your eyes while expressing disapproval of the way a harsh client is addressing you.
o Beware of crossing the boundaries of respect and regard while smiling or looking at clients who are older, have special needs, or are considered decision makers. Body language for such clients greatly affects their trust in accepting what you say or present in discussions.

Behaviours That Repulse Your Clients

o using your cell phone during discussions
o chewing gum or food, or making noises with your mouth
o rolling over the pen to the client, instead of directly handing it over
o interrupting the client while she speaks
o eating or drinking anything with a pungent smell right before speaking to the client
o tapping your fingers on the table, or allowing body language to slow down your work

The Communication Skills of a Salesperson

Defining the Communication Skills of a Salesperson

The sales profession is considered the profession where communication skills is needed the most. It is through those skills that information, meanings, and ideas are communicated; relationships are created; and discussions are managed, which allows the salesman and the company she works for to achieve their goals and present customers with what suits their needs and exceeds their expectations. This can be accomplished using various tools such as verbal language, body language, presentation tools, and marketing materials.

The Key Elements of Communication

1. sender
2. receiver
3. message content
4. transmission method
5. operations that result from the above elements; for example, negative feedback, the clarity of the transmitted message, and the number of senders and receivers

Types of Communication

All methods that include interaction between two parties are considered types of communication. Nowadays there are various types of communication, but the most important types and methods are as follows:

1. direct interpersonal communication: both parties are seeing and listening to each other directly, and are together in the same place
2. direct communication using different mediums: both parties are seeing and listening to each other directly, but are not in the same place (e.g., video calls)
3. direct, interpersonal, nonverbal communication: both parties are seeing and understanding each other directly and are together in the same place (e.g., people with special needs, military or athletic joint task forces)
4. direct, nonverbal communication using different mediums: both parties are seeing and understanding each other through body language, but they are not in the same place (e.g., in video calls with people with special needs)

Elements of Understanding and Interacting with the Message

Effective communication is primarily based on understanding the content and purpose of the message. For this reason, as a successful salesman, you should have the necessary skills to understand and deal with the message. The most important skills include the following.

1. Listening carefully and attentively.
2. Allowing the sender to convey his message fully, without interrupting or asking questions.
3. Making sure you understand the real meaning of the message.
   - For instance: Mr Abdullah, do you mean ...?
4. Expertly interacting with and responding to the message
5. Organising the content of your reply.
   - For instance: When demonstrating the benefits of a product or service, begin with the benefits and features, and then move on to the pricing.
6. The content of your reply should be limited to addressing what was stated in the original message. Anything beyond this will have a negative impact on the effectiveness of the communication. For example:

Client (while waiting to finish certain procedures): Before coming here, I was at the hospital with my son.

Salesman: Mr Abdullah, would you like to pay in cash or via a debit card?

The Time Management Skills of a Salesperson

Time is a resource that, once used, can never be recovered. If time is not invested properly, you will lose out on the most important elements of your personal success, the success of your business, and achieving your goals. A salesman should pay attention to organising his time, especially while managing his relationships with clients in both the simplest and the most complicated matters, because a salesman should not spend an entire day in just a single step of a million steps that he has to take in the world of sales in order to build his future, make profit for his company, and earn good personal income for himself. Thus, you have to focus on organising your time every day while keeping in mind the duties, roles, and accomplishments that must be achieved and attained. This can be performed though the following:

- identifying the time needed for getting yourself ready
- identifying the exact time when you will close off your working day, according to procedures and regulations
- identifying the timings of the client visits, if you are a field salesman
- identifying the time required to achieve your daily, monthly, and annual sales targets
- identifying the time required to accomplish the five steps of a sales operation and then move on to serve another client
- identifying the time required to prepare your surroundings and the things you might need in the place you meet your clients
- identifying the time that you need to set aside to attend to personal matters, such as prayers, lunch, and rest

Aspects of Managing the Finances of a Salesperson

Managing financials is one of the most important matters of our lives, and it will not be effective unless we are highly committed and very accurate. This matter is even more important to a salesman because he is the link between several financial areas, the most important of which are:

- financial responsibility
- company property
- the value of the company's products
- daily income from profit

- money paid by clients in return for products or services

Neglecting any of those areas would mean that a salesman is jeopardising his future and his level of income, and it will increase his liabilities towards his company in the future.

There are general guidelines that can help the salesman organise his financials and steer clear of risks, the most important of which are the following:

- committing to the exact time of daily financial close
- committing to the company's procedures and regulations
- accurately counting the money received before the start of the workday
- making sure of the authenticity of money bills according to the procedures or devices approved by the company
- accurately counting the money received from a client and double-checking the amount when depositing it
- not being tolerant or lenient with your team, no matter what the situation is, when it comes to financial matters
- never placing money, receipts, or financial statements in an place not assigned to them
- if the working day is split into two shifts, being sure to follow the regulations and procedures when it comes to handing over and receiving money
- making sure not to mix up personal money with the company's money, no matter what the reasons are

The Eleven Salesman's Preparation and Daily Reviews That Help Him Maintain His Success

There are some tasks that are considered essential for a salesman to perform every day before meeting his clients in order to maintain his excellent performance and continue being successful in the world of sales.

1. reviewing the latest information
2. getting prepared by setting his goals for the day, and how he plans to achieve these goals
3. reviewing the latest updates and developments in procedures and regulations
4. checking the cleanliness of his surroundings/office and making sure it is organised and ready to receive clients
5. going over his achievements and the weak and strong points of the previous day's performance
6. attending to personal hygiene (breath, clothes, body odour, etc.)
7. making sure that all presentation tools such as marketing flyers, samples, and contracts are available

8. making sure that all stationery such as pens and notepads is available
9. reviewing the latest updates and developments at the company, especially the ones related to the products and services that he is responsible for marketing and selling
10. psychologically preparing for being creative in the job by, for example, arriving early to the place where he will be spending his working hours
11. attending the morning meetings with his team to discuss and share opinions; this will help him overcome any weak points in the previous day's performance and maintain an excellent performance in the new day

The Skills and Personal Interests of a Successful Salesperson

All successful and professional salespeople across the world who wholeheartedly love their career and do not simply regard it as a job have certain skills and personal interests in common. Some interests might be part of their daily tasks, but below we will shed some light on those interests that lie outside the salesman's job duties.

The most important skills and personal interests include the following:

- ✓ extremely patient
- ✓ acute sense of observation and focus
- ✓ ability to understand things quickly
- ✓ always willing to put in extra effort
- ✓ care for others and love for attracting attention
- ✓ ability to get and hold the attention of others
- ✓ love of precision and organisation in their personal quests and journeys
- ✓ very sociable; prefer team sports
- ✓ highly cooperative in both their personal and professional lives
- ✓ simplicity in way the way they dress and in their lives in general
- ✓ acceptance for others, no matter how different their education or inclinations are
- ✓ love games that are based on reasoning and use of one's intellect
- ✓ love of exploration, discovery, and advancing and developing their skills
- ✓ experts in presentation and in ways of verbally demonstrating benefits and flaws
- ✓ benefit from their own experiences as well as others' experiences; like to talk about those experiences
- ✓ love diversity in what they own; you often find them owning more than one brand of a certain product
- ✓ always have the desire to sell and to talk about selling, products, and services
- ✓ have a strong sense of belonging to their companies and show great loyalty when speaking about them

The Sixteen Types and Behaviours of Clients

The types and behaviours of clients vary, whether intentionally or not, according to different psychological, social, or cultural factors. You have to respect all those factors and aspects and be perfectly capable of dealing with them for the following reasons:

1. to save your time and the time of your client
2. to give clients a genuine opportunity to make their own decisions
3. to provide them with a better and more appealing service
4. to maintain effective communication with all your clients
5. to fairly give them the optimal alternatives that best suits their needs
6. to be able to understand the real needs of the clients, regardless of their types or behaviours

With time, as you become an expert in dealing with those types, you will discover that selling has become more enjoyable, and that your client base is constantly becoming bigger and more supportive.

The Most Widespread Types/Behaviours/Psychological Conditions

1. **The friend**
   - never accepts lies
   - does not like praise or compliments
   - flexible; accepts advice and guidance
   - always looking for additional services
   - can speak about any topic in general
   - does not really care about the price of what he will get, if he truly wants to have it
   - does not care much about time, but hates waiting as well
   - is cheerful and smiley, believes that he can be friends with everybody and that no one will harm him, and sees the world as a perfect place
   - always wants the products and services that support working with others and that do not hinder his daily and social activities

The Most Important Keys to Dealing with a Friend

- Seize any opportunity of agreement, and have it lead to a friendlier and closer relationship.
- Do not trail off your conversation with him while working on closing off the transaction, no matter how busy you are.
- Maintain a cheerful body language and present him with product offers during his waiting time.
- Do not lose your smile or hospitality, regardless of how awkward or embarrassing the outcomes of the discussions were for you.

- Always take control of the conversation; this means that you will be constantly steering back to the main topic of discussion about the product or service.
- Never undermine the topics he brings up; try to control your body language, especially your facial expressions.
- Do not unprofessionally lead him to close off a topic or to focus on the topic of the products or services that he wants to purchase.
- Be careful while speaking and dealing with him, for he is very honest and believes that honesty is one of his rights, irrespective of whether what he says seems unfair to you or your company.

2. **The one with rough behaviour**
   - nervous and irritable
   - others fear him because of his maltreatment
   - stubborn and opinionated, even if he was mistaken
   - always trying to distort what he wants to purchase in order to get it for the lowest price
   - cares a great deal about the amount of money he is going to pay and the benefits he will receive in return
   - believes that his personal worth or value is determined by how roughly he treats people, whether through words, a loud voice, or slander

The Most Important Keys to Dealing with the One with Rough Behaviour

- Present your products and services with utmost confidence, and do not hesitate or falter while answering any of his questions.
- Always appear serious while accepting his remarks, but avoid discussing them in-depth.
- Seize any opportunity of agreement and have it lead the client into becoming more positive during the conversation.
- Try not to smile often; be more serious. However, be careful not to totally lose your smile.
- Accept any negative behaviour, and try to immediately and expertly identify his needs.
- After identifying the need, begin with explaining the most important benefits that he will get from using the product or service.
- As much as possible, stay away from comparing your own products or services with the ones he currently has, even if he attempts to do so.
- Maintain serious eye contact and a serious body language throughout the discussion; show him interest and attention.
- Always ignore his negative verbal or physical behaviour, such as banging his fist on the table or generally attacking the company.

3. **The talkative**
   - does not listen to you properly
   - talking a lot, even about trivial matters, is how he presents the importance of his personality
   - often selects or chooses a product or service but speaks about the benefits of something else
   - speaks freely in a way that might cross the personal boundaries of others, regardless of how sensitive the topics he speaks about are
   - you need to utilise all your capabilities and skills in managing the discussion and making it focus on the crux of the matter
   - brings up discussions in a variety of areas; however, his discussions are often pointless and aimless
   - speaks to anyone around him, with no exception; that is, he speaks with any person who can hear him, regardless of whether he knows this person

The Most Important Keys to Dealing with the Talkative

   - Organise your time properly.
   - Keep very good track of your time; he can be willing to spend his whole day talking with you.
   - Seize any opportunity of agreement, and make it a controlling point by which you can get back your handle on the discussion.
   - Be smart and tactful; make him feel how important it is for you to serve him and serve other clients as well.
   - Gently and professionally try to remind him that there are others waiting for your help, without making him notice how talkative he is.
   - It is his right, like that of any other client, that you never lose your temper for any reason. Make sure he is listening attentively while you present the points that support his choice of purchasing what suits his needs.
   - Understand his needs by constantly asking indirect polar (yes-no) questions, such as:
   - Mr (…), is your cellular line account prepaid or postpaid? (Instead of asking him what type of cellular line account he has.)
   - Always acknowledge what he says, but professionally steer back to the crux of the topic. For example:
        * Client: Do you like football?
        * Salesman: Yes. Would you like to have the mobile phone Internet service that allows you to watch the most important goals of your favourite team?
   - Be careful not to deal with him in a negative attitude after you are done with the selling and purchasing operation, even if the operation was for any reason unsuccessful. Do not behave negatively, either verbally or with your body language. This is a grave mistake that will lead to losing this client in the future.

4. **The decision maker**
   - knows exactly what he wants
   - stubborn and proud of himself
   - never allows others to make decisions on his behalf
   - always recounts stories about successful decisions he has made
   - constantly tries to make you feel that he is different from others
   - performs his own research about the products and services before discussing them with you
   - ambitious and very knowledgeable about what he wants to purchase or discuss
   - gives examples to make you feel that he is able to choose and make decisions
   - never accepts being advised to take a certain decision, even if this decision was in his favour
   - takes responsibility for his own decisions, does not accept blame for and does not justify his choices
   - has already determined what he wants beforehand but visits and speaks with you just to make sure that his choice is correct
   - never argues about anything that he does not have adequate information about; tells you that he needs to research the subject before making a specific decision
   - does not buy on impulse; however, he is impulsive in making the correct decision, even if the purchase gets delayed because he is still making more comparisons

The Most Important Keys to Dealing with the Decision Maker

- Listen to him attentively while he explains what he wants.
- Answer all his questions with full confidence and with correct and precise information.
- Respect his point of view about your products or services, whether it is positive or negative.
- Keep a serious smile and maintain a respectful body language while dealing with him.
- Seize any opportunity of agreement, and concur with his decision and the benefits that he will receive as a result of this decision.
- Acknowledge all his comments, complaints, or objections expertly and formally. For example:
  - Client: This branch is very crowded and unorganised.
  - Salesman: Thank you. I respect your opinion, and I will communicate it to those in charge. I hope you allow me to give your mobile phone number to the upper management so that they can discuss with you your valuable comments.
- Keep track of time throughout the conversation and while finalising the sales operation. This personality greatly respects those who respect time.
- Never try to free yourself from responsibility when accused or blamed for something, even if it is not directly related to your work in products and services.

- Do not present many options. This will bother him and make him feel that you are unable to understand his needs.
- Never try to change his decision about purchasing a product or service after he has already made the decision. Try to professionally propose to reexplain he benefits and features of this product or service.
- Always use logic and reasoning while speaking with him. Stay clear from persuasion. If you are unable to do so, ask another colleague to serve him. However, beware of jeopardising your relationship with him by using something other than logic in your conversations.

5. **The hesitant**
   - never makes impulsive decisions
   - does not care much about time; he even uses it as an excuse to avoid taking decisions
   - always expresses his liking for the product or service but rarely decides to purchase it
   - always compares between different services and prices; avoids being persuaded to making a particular choice
   - if you are able to determine his needs and give him what he wants, he will be the best client who can market for you and your company
   - usually speaks positively about products and services even though he might not own any
   - looks for someone who can provide him with alternatives but also needs someone who can support his decision; he is always passionate and ambitious
   - does not care much for the price of the product or service he decides to purchase, although price was one of the reasons for his hesitance in making the decision
   - earning his satisfaction is very important and beneficial for you because he considers your support for him in making his decisions a huge favour that deserves to be told to all those around him
   - does not have confidence in his choices or ability to choose; thus, you will find it very difficult to earn his trust because he is constantly looking for more clarification to the reasons of why he should choose a particular product or service

The Most Important Keys to Dealing with the Hesitant

- Help him make his decision, but never try to decide for him.
- Patience is the key factor; understanding and trying to determine the choice is the second factor.
- Do not concur with his comparisons between other companies and the offers and benefits they provide. Instead, become an expert in presenting what distinguishes you from others.
- Seize any opportunity of agreement and allow this to help you determine his needs. Demonstrate the benefits, characteristics, and after-sale services of the very first thing he selects and accepts to purchase.

- Be patient and do not lose your temper if you find yourself repeating the different steps of the sales operation more than once. For example:
  - Client: I want a product that costs 100 Riyals.
  - Salesman: Here you go. This product costs 100 Riyals and suits your needs.
  - Client: Please accept this payment.
  - Salesman: Shall I start filling out the sales form?
  - Client: Hold on. Will I be able to exchange this product in the future?
  - Salesman: Yes you can, but this is this year's latest production.
  - Client: I am not sure … Can I see another product, even if it is for a higher or lower price?
  - Salesman: Here you go. These are two more products that almost suit your needs.
  - Client: No, I want more expensive products, but ones with extra benefits.
  - Salesman: Here you go. I hope this product suits your needs.
  - Client: I need a chance to think. I might go back and purchase the first product that cost 100 Riyals.
- You have to answer his queries. However, keep track of the time and of your progress in determining his needs.
- Never force him into making a particular decision. Instead, be honest in guiding him to the choice that best suits his needs.

6. **The positive**
   - responsive; very calm
   - rarely gets nervous or agitated
   - responds to all arguments
   - manages discussions effectively
   - his first impression is positive
   - has listening and negotiation skills
   - accepts another view if it was better than his; can change his opinion or decision
   - finds excuses to anyone who does him wrong
   - does not accept anything unless it makes sense to him
   - accepts views and rapidly evaluates them
   - his criticisms and objections are based on positive arguments and constructive criticism

The Most Important Keys to Dealing with the Positive

- Always show positivity when dealing with him.
- Your body language should be positive and friendly.
- Smile; do not overact in your behaviours, words, or body language.
- A positive client gets emotionally affected if addressed in a nonpositive way.
- Be careful not to point out to him that his positive view is wrong. For example:
  - Client: Your competitor has an advantage of making discounts on long-distance calls.

○ No, no, no ... You just don't understand their policy in exploiting the customers. Their prices for local calls are higher than ours, and that is why they reduce the prices of long-distance calls.

- Always be reasonable and logical with him; do not speak about topics that are not related to the topic of discussion.
- Do not raise your voice while trying to draw his attention to a benefit or a feature.
- Do not reject his opinion, even if it was unrelated to the topic or contains inaccurate information. Instead, try to professionally correct him.
- If he shows liking or acceptance of a certain positive aspect of the product or service, seize the opportunity and explain how this positive aspect is compatible with his needs and provides added value and benefit.
- Be well-versed with your information and remain positive about all comparisons that come up during the discussion. Do not criticise your competitors or mention their downsides, even if they are true.

7. **The one with special needs**
- determined
- confident
- well-versed about what he wants to purchase
- does not usually like to be treated differently
- likes to wait for his turn and follow procedures and regulations
- first-class speaker; knows very well the basics of effective communication
- does not accept being pitied or treated in a way that derogates his potential and abilities

The Most Important Keys to Dealing with the One with Special Needs

- You, as well as the company you work for, should serve and respect him.
- You should commit to our duty in giving him his full rights without making him feel pitied in any way.
- Do not commit the grave mistake of asking him about how he lives with his disability.
- Control your body language very well; do not bend when serving him except under special conditions. Respect his determination, for he is the knight of determination.
- Never focus on his disability, whether it is a physical or verbal.
- Avoid the repetitive offer to help; he might interpret your actions as pity, which is absolutely unacceptable.
- If you find him satisfied that your products or services are compatible with his needs, seize this opportunity to fully explain the features and benefits that will best suit his needs.

- Provide him with all the means of comfort. However, try your best to do this without making him feel that you are treating him any differently from others.

8. **The egoist**
   - loves recognition
   - very conceited
   - does not care much about the money he spends in order to satisfy his ego
   - gets very angry if his ego is detracted
   - very particular about his possessions and tries his best to show them off
   - believes that he is entitled to have everything, even if he is not
   - always boasts about his possessions, decisions, and personal matters
   - believes that everybody around him should admire his behaviour, possession, words, and body language
   - has a psychological state that makes him believe that everything he owns is very valuable and should be admired by all people around him
   - vanity is not a result of financial status, like wealth of poverty; it is a psychological state that we have to accept and deal with, without questioning (e.g., 'Why is this man so conceited?')

The Most Important Keys to Dealing with the Egoist

- Never let go of your smile.
- Do not seek to take revenge against his ego.
- Do not get angry or agitated; stay calm.
- Show that you are impressed by what he says; however, do not lose control over the discussion.
- Deal with him and attract his interest through the perspective that represents his egoistic side.
- Never try to exploit his ego by pushing him into purchasing expensive products and services that he might not need.
- Though his body language is often provocative, try to accept it; understand that it is a psychological state that should be dealt with.
- Seize any moment in which he 'forgets' his ego, and continue to understand his needs and present him with the best alternatives.
- Express admiration for what he is trying to show you but without going into details. For example:
  - Client: I just purchased this watch a while ago. It is very big. It is expensive, but it is very big.
  - Salesman: Wow. It is lovely and worth buying. Excuse me, Mr X, which of these products better fits into your monthly spending?
- Accept his comments and be persistent in presenting your goods and services; always give praise and compliments, but in a professional way
- Do not show lack of interest when he speaks arrogantly about his personal matters. This might decrease the friendly tone of your conversation.

- Do not expect him to express any appreciation for you or for what you present. This type of client never shows that he is impressed with anything, even if he truly is.

9. **The rushing client**
   - lacks patience
   - hates to wait
   - lacks focus what he truly needs
   - likes to be loud and disturb other clients in the waiting room
   - likes to be the only client accommodated and cared for
   - always wants to have things quickly, even if it is incompatible with his needs
   - always wants to have things quickly, even if it means paying extra
   - talks constantly about how busy he is in order to speed up his procedures and get quick feedback, which is usually not positive
   - never waits for his turn; comes straight up to the salesperson even if there are other clients waiting to be served or are being serviced

The Most Important Keys to Dealing with the Rushing Client

- Do not respond to his tempers and rush. Instead, try to understand him and deal with him professionally.
- Explain to him that the matter will not take much time, but do not promise that it will be rushed.
- If he expresses his liking for a certain product, seize the opportunity and make sure it suits his needs by going over its benefits and features. Then start finalising the procedure.
- Maintain your calmness and your positive body language. Due to his rushing nature, he never sees how much effort you are putting to help him. He will try to bring up the issue of time verbally or through his body language (e.g., looking at the clock or constantly changing his seating position).
- Try to divert his attention from wanting to quickly be done with his procedures to his surroundings. For example:
  - ○ Client: I want to purchase this product.
  - ○ Salesman: I am here to assist you. Please give me a chance to finish my work with Mr … (At this point, create a visual contact with the client to whom you are speaking.)
- Try to calm him down by giving him other interesting things, such as flyers of new products, the chance to try a new product, or a look at new features.

10. **The older client**
   - regards all younger people as his children
   - always speaks of the good times and things of the past
   - wants to try the product or service before purchasing it
   - is the most stable type of client because of his realistic views

- is very experienced in life
- does not accept anything short of respect and appreciation to his generation and their achievements
- cares a great deal about financials, procedures, and systems
- always wants to guide and advise those around him
- does not care much for time; he already set a time in his schedule to meet you
- initially refuses anything new, but might accept it later if it was beneficial, and might even recommend it to others
- might ask you about personal matters, such as your family name, your father's occupation, and whether you are married
- always wants to receive a paper trail for all procedures
- gets very angry if you detract from your respect for him or if you do not respond to his requests, because he regards everybody as his own children

The Most Important Keys to Dealing with the Older Client

- Give him more respect.
- Give him priority.
- Give him more appreciation.
- Give him more acceptance.
- Answer his questions welcomingly.
- Whatever his criticisms are, always accept them with a wide smile.
- Do not offer more features or benefits if he does not need them, just to push him to choose the product.
- Provide him with more details of the features of products and services, as well as the ways to use and benefit from them.
- Treat him as it you are family; make him feel like you are his son and that you are happy to help and provide him with what best suits his needs.
- Never try to undermine his generation and the products and services they used to have, even if he brought this up himself.
- Never make him feel like what he is purchased is too modern and complicated for him; older people have rich life experiences that enable them to learn anything at any time.
- Seize the moment when he wants to try out a product and a service. However, be honest and transparent. Some of them are not familiar with the products or are purchasing them for other people, like their children. Therefore you have to make sure that what he wants to purchase is actually what he needs or what he is looking for.

11. **The shy client**
    - asks only a few questions
    - abides by rules and regulations
    - does not mind waiting
    - rarely asks questions, and his answers are brief

- prefers to deal with people who are shy like him
- does not care much for the price of what he wants
- does not attract attention or focus towards him
- cares about how quickly he is served and understood, even if he does not show it
- always looks at what surrounds the person he is speaking to; never focuses directly on him
- does not care much for extra features or offers on the product or service that he purchased
- never goes off topic; he just wants to get done
- tries to end conversations quickly because he does not like to answer questions or express or discuss his opinions

The Most Important Keys to Dealing with the Shy Client

- Do not try to disregard the importance of showing him respect and appreciation, simply because he is a shy person.
- Do not exploit his shyness and speak to other clients while serving him.
- Do not try to make him become more outgoing, and do not ask him to do so.
- Understand that being shy does not mean being weak; it is merely a personality trait, no more and no less. Note well your body language (the way you look at him, your hands, etc.).
- The shy client likes and responds well with closed-ended questions. For example:
  - Salesperson: Mr X, do you want a product with a three-year guarantee?
  - Client: Yes.
- Avoid using open-ended questions because they confuse the shy client and might make him chose something that he does not need or that does not suit his needs. For example:
  - Salesperson: Mr X, do you want a product with a three-year guarantee, or a product with a two-year guarantee?
  - Client: I am not sure; just give me what is available.
- The shy client has more pride than other types of clients. Do not cross the boundaries of his pride with any inappropriate behaviour.
- If he agrees to purchase any of the alternatives you provided him with, seize the opportunity and start closing off the deal; do not repeat the discussion or reexplain the features and benefits.
- Do not assume that just because he is shy, that he does not understand what you are saying. Do not repeat information or ask him whether he fully understood what you explained.
- His lack of visual contact might make you lose the opportunity of enforcing the importance of what you are presenting through your body language or visual contact. For example:
  - Your big smile and wide eyes while you are trying to highlight the importance of a special feature you are talking about

12. The angry client

Important note: An angry client has two main states.

1. A temporarily angry client: The client was coincidentally angry during the visit. After he calms down, try to figure out what type of client he is, and then concentrate on the best way to deal with him.
2. A constantly angry client: He is always angry, even if he is quiet or does not show any sign of anger. This is one of his traits and personal qualities, and this is what we will discuss below.

The constantly angry client

- does not discuss his decisions
- always sees himself right
- aggressive in his reactions and body language
- is usually nervous; his behaviours are unpredictable
- does not like prolonged conversations, unless he is the one speaking
- always objects, simply to vent out his anger
- hates exaggerated greetings and believes that your smile means that you are undermining his presence and what he is saying
- claims that he is listening attentively to you, but actually he is listening and preparing the question he will ask you the minute you are done
- nothing you present will make him reach the stage where his actions convey satisfaction, even if he is truly and completely satisfied
- uses a very loud voice during conversations; likes to control discussions and topics
- it is very difficult to satisfy him or earn his loyalty
- does not care for the price he will pay for the product as much as he cares for the guarantee that he will receive the exact benefits and features related to the product or service that you discussed

The Most Important Keys to Dealing with the Angry Client

- Do not hesitate while replying to one of his question or while suggesting anything.
- Be patient and control yourself.
- Always use logic while speaking with him; give logical answers to all his questions.
- Maintain a serious body language along with a soft smile, but do not overdo it.
- Use open-ended questions; this will give him some time to calm down while thinking about the answers.
- This type of client will strongly defend you and your company if you are able to truly earn his loyalty and trust.
- Your first reaction to his anger would be to accept responsibility for what he is complaining about and to express your absolute readiness to solve the issue that is making him angry.

- It is imperative that you avoid giving out wrong information during discussions. This type of client considers your mistakes a chance to attack you and to take control over the discussion.
- Resolving or attending to the client's objections, complaints, or bad past experiences that make him angry are golden opportunities to earn his loyalty.
- Seize the time when he gets calm after you suggest to him the most suitable alternatives or solutions to the problems that are making him angry; being quiet and not asking questions indicates that he has initially accepted those alternatives and solutions.
- Keep track of time; the more time that passes without serving him or having him reach the stage of accepting or rejecting the alternatives that you presented him with, the higher the chance that his anger will mount, which eventually means you will lose the opportunity of winning him as a client.
- Take responsibility for whatever is making him angry. Face it and deal with it professionally, and take the proper procedures to solve any issues—even if the issues are not your or your team's responsibilities and are the responsibilities of other departments. However, do not begin solving those issues except after fully explaining the solutions to the angry client and clarifying the reasons behind needing to take such actions.

13. **The visiting client**
   - not serious
   - always asks about future offers
   - is not enthusiastic or interested in what you suggest
   - is not looking for anything specific to purchase
   - is interested in knowing the prices, packages, and products in general
   - likes to watch from a distance rather than inquire directly or ask questions
   - is interested in product accessories and services more than he is about the actual product or service
   - focuses on the products and services and their advertisements rather than on salespeople
   - makes quick comparisons and focuses on highlighting the benefits and features of the products and services that he already owns
   - coincidence, curiosity, passing time, and advertisements are some of the reasons for his visit
   - collects flyers of products and services in order to read them later; however, he does not ask the salespeople directly for them

The Most Important Keys to Dealing with the Visiting Client

- Always begin the conversation with the product that mostly attracted his attention.
- Insist on attracting his interest and attention; act professionally.
- Do not make the visiting client feel like he is being monitored or followed.

- If he asks about a product or service, start by stating the strongest features and benefits without mentioning its price.
- If you make eye contact with him, start with a professional and welcoming body and verbal language, but do not get physically too close to him.
- Offer to explain any feature, product, or service available on the marketing flyers.
- Give him the marketing flyers of any product he asks about to allow him a bigger chance of becoming interested in the product or service when he goes back to his house or goes out with his friends.
- If you find him seriously attracted to a certain product or service, or showing interest when talking about it or while answering one of your casual questions, seize the opportunity and try to understand his needs. Do this by stating the features and benefits of your products and services.
- Give him a reason to think about your products and services and to return to you later. This can be done by giving him such things as marketing flyers, explaining to him future offers and features, or informing him about the time when discounted products and services will be available.

14. The client who claims knowledge
- always says 'I know'
- is sure of himself and his information, even if the information is wrong
- does not give you the chance to finish what you are saying during discussions
- does not listen attentively, and even when he does, he always restates what he knows
- is generally informed; that is, he reads titles but not the content
- always 'threatens' others by claiming that he knows information, is well-informed, and is able to evaluate things properly
- speaks about everything, whether or not it's related to the topic of discussion
- always tries to undermine the value of the information you have or the suggestions you give during discussions
- cares a great deal about the price he will pay, more so than he does about the benefits and features he will receive
- uses his information to try to take control and command of the conversation, irrespective of whether the information is correct or not
- this type of client is extremely loyal, to the extent that he might give out wrong information about you simply to prove that you are the best

The Most Important Keys to Dealing with the Client Who Claims Knowledge

- Note your body language, especially as more time passes.
- Refrain from asking him about the validity of his information.
- Always accept what he says; if he asks any questions, always give the correct answer, even if it might contradict what he says.

- Refrain from trying to prove what you say; always attribute the information you present to its sources.
- Spend your time with the client professionally; this type of client asks about everything in general without getting into specifics, simply to be able to speak about them later.
- If you find him interested in a product or service that he claims to know all about, seize the opportunity, try to understand his needs, and present him with the most suitable alternatives.
- Avoid comparing yourself with your competitors; he is generally informed about the competitors' products and services. However, to prove the validity of his information, he might give you incorrect details simply to make you lose your control over the discussion.

15. **The important client (VIP)**
- listens attentively
- cares a lot about time
- cares a lot about the smallest details
- confident; a decision maker
- does not purchase anything beyond what he actually needs
- looks for what would satisfy both his current as well as his future needs
- does not like to get into discussions; likes conversations to be specific and concise
- prefers to be distinct and unique; does not care about the amount of money he spends in return for this uniqueness
- regards and deals with everything as an investment; views all what is around him as an opportunity for a future investment, including his relationships, possessions, and decisions

The Most Important Keys to Dealing with the Important Client

- Save both your time and his time.
- Be more welcoming and display more hospitality protocols.
- Do not prolong while presenting your products or services.
- Speak about the advantage of your pricing at the very end of the discussion.
- Do not keep him waiting without clarifying the reason for the delay.
- Do not commit to anything you won't be able to fulfil, even if it was the responsibility of another department.
- If he agrees to purchase one of the alternatives, begin the procedures immediately; never open up the conversation or even a part of the conversation again. This type of client knows exactly what to choose and does not take any decision unless he is fully convinced with the features and benefits of what he chose.

16. Dealing with Women (Maintaining Both Privacy and Professionalism)

Our Islamic culture is our primary support and is the main reason why a woman should be treated in a sophisticated and constructive way, all within the framework of maintaining the utmost respect for her privacy and the characteristics bestowed upon her by Allah SWT. A women client may be classified as or have the behaviours of one of the client types described above. When it comes to women, however, the difference lies in those areas where she should be especially cared for and respected. This applies in managing the selling relationships and in all other areas discussed in this booklet.

The Most Important Keys to Dealing with a Woman

- **Never invade her privacy. For example,** staring at her eyes or hands. When answering her questions, always look at her quickly and casually and direct your look towards the area around her eyes, but beware of focusing on her eyes.
- Avoid excessive smiles or loud laughs.

- **When serving her, always give her priority and privacy.** For example, determine a special waiting place, try to quickly finish the procedures required for her request, and so on.

- **Maintain her trust.** For example, when making a copy of her ID, try not to show her picture.
- As much as possible, avoid speaking about your personal matters, even if you were asked to do so.
- Do not try to test the product or to explain its benefits using anything that belongs to the woman.
- Maintain a serious body language.
- If you need a phone number to finalise the procedures, ask for the number of one of her relatives, such as that of her husband, father, or son—not her personal number.

- **Keep an intermediate object to avoid direct interaction.** For example, do not directly hand her a pen; place it on the table, where her hands can reach it.
- When clarifying anything on the sales contract, do not explain while the contract is still in her hands. Take the contract (intermediate object) and ask her about the point she wants clarified. Read it off the contract that is now in your hands and explain to her what she wants to know.
- Never extend your hand to welcome her or to offer to shake her hand.
- Beware of looking at her or following her with your eyes while she is leaving the place.
- Be very careful in choosing your words during the conversation. Note your body language. A woman will not accept the same level of friendliness or hospitality

that we use with men, because this is considered a breach and violation to the privacy, respect, and appreciation with which she should be treated.

The First Impression Skill

The concept of first impression refers to those first few seconds where your abilities, skills, physical appearance, body language, good behaviour, and skill in maintaining eye contact and active listening with the client collectively leave an effect on him. The importance of the effect of the first impression is highlighted in the answers to the following questions.

❖ Does the effect support your credibility and honesty with your client?

❖ Did the effect create you the image that you actually wanted your clients to have of you?

❖ Did the effect result in creating a new positive relationship with the client? Will it create more opportunities for opening up new conversations with him?

❖ Did the effect make you willingly accept the presence of your client around you? Did it make you happy to serve him?

❖ Did the effect allow you to accomplish the first step (the opening) through to the final step (the closure)?

The importance of the first impression lies in its direct effect on the customer's trust as well as his willingness to continue in his relationship with you from the beginning up until the end. I labelled this as a skill because even though you might have many positive abilities, if you lack the skill of managing them all, they will never support your relationship with your client or affect the degree to which he accepts you.

The Basics of Making a Great First Impression

Below are a few guidelines to help you leave a strong and positive impact on your client within the first few seconds of meeting him.

o Your clothes reflect your personality.
  – Beware not to go too easy or to overdo this.

  – Focus on what adds more formality and confidence.

o Become an expert and excel in your verbal communication skills.
  – Maintain a calm and enthusiastic tone of voice.

  – Maintain a logical period of silence between your words and sentences.

– Make sure that the message you want to send to the client is very clear. (If you do not want to speak in classical Arabic, then avoid using colloquial and ambiguous terms.)

o Become an expert and excel in your physical communication skills.
– Avoid exaggerating your body language.

– Maintain a body language that combines confidence and cordialness.

– Do not get physically too close to your clients; avoid touching them as much as possible.

o Become an expert and excel in your visual communication skills.
– Do not ignore those who accompany the client, such as the father or a friend. Maintain your respect for them.

– Read, learn, and practice this skill very well; it sends very effective messages, which may be either positive or negative.

– Note where you direct your look while speaking to your clients. Do not look at the floor, do not look at another client, and do not look at the place where the client is injured or has a physical defect.

o Do not allow psychological, work, or personal pressures to affect your image with the client.
– Do not ignore a client's smile because of the way he behaves or because you are busy with another client.

– Even if surrounded by a large number of clients, do not forget to note and care for your clothes and the way you look.

– Beware not to let the pressures you face be exposed through your body language, such as speaking with a hoarse or tired voice, looking at people in a way that indicates lack of sleep, or moving very slowly in a way that shows how exhausted you are.

The Basics of Visual Communication Skills

- Always look at the eyes of the person with whom you are speaking.
- Control your body language during visual communication; keep them both in positive sync with each other.

- Always look at your client in a nice and friendly way. Do not look at him in an offensive way or in a way that might result in a nonpositive reaction, such as anger, boredom, or disregard.
- Avoid looking at your clients for either a very short or a very long period of time; the former might show that you are unfriendly, and the latter might indicate that you are confused or tense.
- Never look at a person to show him that you are being attentive while your hands are busy with your mobile phone or pen, or your body language is inappropriate. Do not smile at a person to show that you are welcoming him while your eyes are indicating something else.
- While speaking to a client, do not look upwards or downwards. This might have several effects on the client; he might not trust what you say, he might believe that you do not have an accurate answer, or he might feel that you are ignoring him.
- Visual communication is a tool that can support you in understanding the client's needs through expertly monitoring your client's body language. However, this can be achieved under two conditions:
  1. not losing eye contact during visual communication
  2. not focusing or staring on any of the client's body parts; this may have a nonpositive effect on many clients
- Always maintain positive visual contact with everybody around you, including your current client and the clients who are waiting.
- Never look at your clients while wearing sunglasses or eyeglasses with coloured lenses; both will result in a loss of effective visual communication and may negatively affect the nature of the conversation.

The Five Key Steps for Sales Success

These five key steps are the gifts I always present to the people whom I get the honour to train in the world of sales. Thankfully, I have watched the people I train successfully implement the steps. I ask Allah SWT to grant them to you for your continuous success.

1. introduction
2. understanding and determining the need
3. presenting choices and alternatives
4. ensuring you know and understand the need
5. closure

1. Introduction

Goals of this step:

- Create a common ground for the conversation.
- Succeed in making a great first impression.

- Show respect and hospitality during the client's visit.
- Overcome the psychological boundary between you and the client.
- Show the client how important he is to you and to the company.
- Discover what type of client a person is according to his behaviour.
- Create a foundation for succeeding in the second step, beginning to understand the client's needs, and providing him with alternatives which satisfy those needs.
- Try to use plurals during your conversation to show more respect, but do this professionally. For example: 'We are here to serve you. We provide you with ...' However, note that not everything can be said using plurals.

The basic elements of the 'Introduction' step:

- determining the type of client
- learning the client's name
- expressing you willingness to understand his needs and address his objections
- establishing a friendly and interactive relationship with your client
- expressing your willingness to provide him with the choices and alternatives that best suit his needs
- confidently introducing yourself and your company to the client, even if he is already a long-term client
- choosing the best method with which you should accomplish the remaining steps, and selecting the best location where you can do so

The beginning of a conversation that includes the five steps. (You may use terms from local dialects during the conversation, but do so carefully and make sure the words are clear, easy to understand, and friendly.)

- **Salesman:** Welcome to our company.
- **Client:** Thank you.
- **Salesman:** I am Abdullah, a sales consultant.
- **Client:** Thank you, Abdullah.
- **Salesman:** Excuse me, sir. Please be seated. How can I help you?
- **Client:** Thank you.
- **Salesman:** May I know your name, please?
- **Client:** I am Dr Sultan.

If a client provides a title with his name, such as professor, doctor, or engineer, do not drop off this title while addressing him during the conversation. In this example, continue addressing the client as Dr Sultan.

Things to avoid in this step:

- not knowing the name of your client
- not introducing yourself or your company to the client
- exaggerating your behaviour, words, or body language
- not being able to earn your client's trust or to break the boundary between him and you

- not standing to greet your client, or shaking his hands without smiling and looking confidently at his eyes
- not being able to make your client feel important, or making him feel that you are unable to attend to his needs
- not attending to your personal hygiene and appearance or to the cleanliness and organisation of your desk and the surroundings of the place in which you are going to meet him

2. Learning and Understanding Needs or Objections

Goals of this step:

- identifying the client's needs or objection
- understanding the nature of his use of the products and services that are similar to those you provide
- maintaining the friendly relationship by showing more respect and appreciation
- continuing to invest in your success in making a great first impression (Step 1, Introduction)
- determining how much money the client usually puts aside for such products and services
- understanding in a professional way why the client decided to choose you or to go back to you again, and dealing expertly with the reasons he gives
- creating a foundation for succeeding in the third step, and beginning to suggest options that suit the client's needs or that address his objections

The basic elements of the 'Understanding and Determining the Need/Objection' step:

- determining the client's preferences
- clearly identifying his needs
- using open-ended question to initially determine the needs
- committing to taking necessary and immediate actions to address his objections
- using closed-ended questions (which are typically answered with a yes or a no)
- earning the client's trust; making him feel that you are his personal consultant who is able to attend to his needs, and not merely a salesman
- understanding what the client liked and what he disliked or refused in similar products and services, whether produced by the company itself or by competitors

This conversation includes the five steps.
- **Salesman:** Hello, Dr Sultan. How can I help you?
- **Client:** Thank you. What new products or services do you have?
- **Salesman:** Dr Sultan, do you need a product or a service? (open-ended question)
- **Client:** I would like to purchase a product.

- **Salesman:** Dr Sultan, we have new special products. However, allow me to ask you something. Do you prefer to pay in monthly instalments? (Closed-ended question)
- **Client:** Yes.
- **Salesman:** Dr Sultan, how much do you expect to pay, or how much money have you already set aside for such a product?
- **Client**: About 100 Riyals every month.

Now that the need has been determined and you know how much the client is ready to pay every month, you are ready to proceed with the step of 'Presenting Choices and Alternatives'.

Things to avoid in this step:

- not listening attentively to the client
- losing your smile and enthusiasm during the conversation
- rushing to understand the needs of the client or the reasons behind his objections
- not being able to positively deal with the type and behaviour of the client
- asking the client some personal questions without getting his permission first
- overusing open-ended questions and not being able to control the discussion or the time spent with the client
- presenting the client with choices and alternatives before understanding his real needs or the reasons behind his objections

3. Presenting Choices and Alternatives

Goals of this step:

- expertly providing the client with the most suitable choices and alternatives
- making the client reach the stage of choosing a particular good or service
- saving time and giving the client all means of support and for helping him to make a decision
- proving to your client that he was right in trusting you to supply him with what best suits his needs
- beginning to impress your client with your professionalism, and starting to earn the his trust in and loyalty towards the company
- proving to the client that you can genuinely understand his needs and that you are really able to help him
- presenting the features of the product or service and the benefits of using them in a way that satisfies the client's needs
- creating a foundation for succeeding in the fourth step, and beginning to ensure that you understand the needs of the client in order to proceed with the steps of the actual sale

The basic elements of the 'Presenting Choices and Alternatives' step:

- Do not provide the client with choices and alternatives that leave him confused and make him lose confidence in your ability to understand his needs.
- Present your client with a maximum of two choices and alternatives which suit his needs (that is, if you did not find exactly what he needs).
- The two choices always are:
  ○ a product or service that is a little less than what the client needs (there is a probability that the client might increase his use later, or he might need more features than what he currently has)
  ○ a product or services that is a little more than what the client needs (the client will never increase his use or need more features that what he currently has)

This conversation includes the five steps.

- **Salesman**: Dr Sultan, do you need the … feature in the product? This will provide you with the following benefits ….
- **Client**: Yes.
- **Salesman**: So, Dr Sultan, according to the amount you set aside for similar products, which is 100 Riyals monthly, and according to our need for the extra feature, I can suggest two choices which would satisfy your needs the most.
  ○ A product that will cost you 110 Riyals monthly, and includes the feature you want in addition to …
  ○ A product that will cost you 90 Riyals monthly, and includes a feature that would provide you with an almost equal benefit to the one you want.
- **Client**: So, brother Abdullah, I would like to purchase the product that costs 110 Riyals.
- **Salesman**: It is an honour to have you choose one of our products.

Because we succeeded in giving the client the choice that best suits his needs, we have earned his trust as well as his loyalty. We now move to the step of making sure that we understand this need and proceed with the procedures.

Things to avoid in this step:

- Do not push your client towards making a particular choice, no matter what the reasons are.
- Do not begin with discussing the price of the product or service; always start with explaining its features and the benefits of its use.
- Avoid getting into personal details; be smart enough to understand the client's need without asking too man personal questions.
- No matter how difficult it is for you to know and understand the needs of the client, never let go of your smile or your positive body language.
- It is a client's right to change his mind. The nature of his needs might also change at any point in time. If this happens, it is your duty to repeat this step or the step of 'Understanding and Determining the Need/Objection' without becoming bored or allowing this to impact your positive attitude or nature of communication.

4. Ensuring You Know and Understand the Need:

Goals of this step:

- ensuring that the client is able to pay for the product or service he chooses to buy
- ensuring that the client is able to satisfy all legal requirements to complete the selling process and to follow the procedures
- ensuring that the client has actually chosen what he needs, and doing so in a professional manner to leave the client without any doubt that he has made the correct choice
- ensuring that the features of the product or service are very clear to the client, and that he fully understands the benefits of its use and knows exactly what services he will receive in return
- ensuring that the client consents to all requirements needed to purchase this product or service (especially in telecommunication companies, car sales, etc.)
- ensuring that the client's selection of the product or service was not influenced by any external factor, and that he did not decide on one of the alternatives you provided without fully understanding the features and benefits of each

The basic elements of the 'Ensuring You Know and Understand the Need' step:

- the client's financial ability
- ensuring that the client's choice actually meets his needs
- ensuring that the client can satisfy all the legal requirements needed to purchase the product or service
- preparing to close the selling process and starting a positive future relationship with the client

The conversation that includes the five steps continues.

- **Salesman**: Dr Sultan, please allow me to ask you a few questions.
- **Client**: Please go ahead.
- **Salesman**: You have chosen this product … that contains the … feature, which will provide you with the following benefits …
- **Client**: Yes.
- **Salesman**: Dr Sultan, this will cost you 110 Riyals. Is this convenient for you?
- **Client**: Yes.
- **Salesman**: Dr Sultan, we need to start preparing the legal contract between yourself and the company. There are some requirements needed, including your national ID, postal code, and email address. Are you able to provide those requirements now?
- **Client**: Yes.
- **Salesman**: Dr Sultan, this will cost 110 Riyals. Are you willing to pay in cash, or do you prefer to use an electronic banking card?
- **Client**: I will pay in cash.

- **Salesman**: Thank you again, Dr Sultan.

Now that we are sure that we have provided the client with a choice that best suits his needs, and that he has the financial and legal ability to continue with the purchase, we have earned the client's trust as well as his increased loyalty. We can now proceed to the 'Closure' step.

Things to avoid in this step:

- nonpositive verbal or visual communication with the client while asking him questions
- assuming that the client clearly understands the features and benefits of what has decided to purchase, and that there is no need to make sure of this once more
- promising that you'll quickly finish the required financial and legal procedures
- using those nonpositive terms when it comes to money, such as:
  - We will take from you the amount of ...
  - You need to pay us the money in order to receive the product.

5. Closure

This step is as important as the 'Introduction' step. Succeeding in making a good first impression has an immediate future effect on you and your company.

Goals of this step:

This final step is a very sensitive step that requires the highest degree of proficiency.

- collecting all legal requirements and following all procedures to close the sale in a perfect way
- preparing the contracts (e.g., information about the client) and financial statements (e.g., receipts)
- fully clarifying to the client the methods and channels of support and help, and the ways of using and benefiting from them
- making sure that the client has no more questions or inquiries
- making sure that the client is absolutely satisfied about all aspects of the selling process (discussions, requirements, etc.)
- ensuring that the client receives all official documents that protect his financial rights and his entitlement for services in the future
- ensuring that the product does not contain any defects before giving it to the client, or making sure of the quality of the service provided to the client before he leaves
- giving the client a wonderful closure that is full of respect and appreciation for his visit and for choosing us to serve him, even if the client did not actually purchase one of your products or services

The basic elements of the 'Closure' step:

- finalising the legal and financial procedures in a way that preserves both the rights of the client and the rights of the company
- making sure the client appreciates the value and importance of his visit and that he understands how grateful and thankful we are for his time and for choosing us
- instilling in clients the confidence in that we are a company that is happy to serve people and is always honoured by their visits, even if they did not purchase any particular product or service
- the way to farewell a client should be full of respect, appreciation, and gratitude for his visit and for the time he spent with us
- ability to earn the client's trust and loyalty through consultative selling rather than persuasive selling

The final part of the conversation that includes the five steps. You may use terms from local dialects during the closure process, but do so carefully, using terms that are clear, easily understood, and gentle.

- Salesman: Dr Sultan, can we kindly have your national ID to make a copy in order to start recording the necessary information on the sales contract?
- Client: Here it is, brother Abdullah.
- Salesman: Thank you, Dr Sultan. Please take back your national ID. This is the copy I made. May you kindly read the terms and conditions of the contract before we start writing the requirements?
- Client: Sure. Thank you, brother Abdullah. I have read the terms and conditions.
- Salesman: Dr Sultan, are the terms and conditions clear? Do you have any questions, or is there any condition that you want me to clarify further?
- Client: Thank you, brother Abdullah. There is no need to do so.
- Salesman: Dr Sultan, please allow us to write the required information together.
- Client: Go ahead, brother Abdullah.
- Salesman: Dr Sultan, we are now done. Can we please review together what has been written?
- Client: Yes. Please go ahead.
- Salesman: Thank you, Dr Sultan. Can you do us the honour of signing here?
- Client: Yes.
- Salesman: Dr Sultan, thank you for your time.
  - This is a copy of the contract.
  - This is a copy of the payment receipt.
  - Please make sure the product does not contain any defects.
- Client: Thank you, brother Abdullah, for your time and effort.
- Salesman: Thank you for visiting us at [company name] and allowing us the opportunity to serve you. It will always be our pleasure to help you.

Things to avoid in this step:

- Asking for anything personal in an inappropriate way, such as the national ID card or an additional mobile number.
- Presenting the terms and conditions in an 'offensive' way that makes the client feel intimated by the company or that the company might have control over him in the future.
- You may fill out the required documents on behalf of the client, but the contract and what you are writing should visible to and reviewed by the client.
- Changing your attitude or body language or not showing the client proper respect and appreciation. This occurs when the client does not purchase a product or service. A positive and elegant closure is a substantial opportunity for a future sale, even if the client did not proceed with the purchase or decided to change his mind and not continue with the purchase for any reason.

References and Readings

- *Secrets of Closing the Sale* by Zig Ziglar
- *The 7 Habits of Highly Effective People: Powerful Lessons in Personal Change* by Stephen R. Covey
- *How to Master the Art of Selling* by Tom Hopkins
- *Secrets of Question Based Selling* by Thomas Freese
- *The Definitive Book of Body Language* by Barbara Pease
- *24 Guidelines for Becoming a Successful Salesperson* by Peter Hoffmann
- *Perfect Selling* by Nick Thornly and Dan Liz
- *How to Attract a Permanent Client* by Dr Talaat Asaad Abdulhameed
- *From Here: Beginning Your Job Stability* by Patrick Forsyth
- *Sales Management and the Art of Selling* by Dr Hassan Ahmed Tawfiq
- *The Personality Compass* by Dayan Turner and Thelma Greco, translation by Hamoud Al-Sharif
- *The Strong Personality: 100 Questions and Answers* by Magdy Kamel
- *The Attractive, Creative, and Effective Personality* by Sobhey Soliman
- *Intelligence and Personality Tests* by Ismail Abdulfattah Abdulkafy
- *The Secrets of Personal Strengths* by Ibrahim Elfiky
- *Know Your Personality* by Amir Taj-ul-dhin

Printed in the United States
By Bookmasters